GROW YOUR AUTHOR PLATFORM:
Copyright © 2019 by Mandi Lynn.

CW00357491

For information contact :
Mandi Lynn: mandi@stoneridgebooks.com
Bethany Atazadeh: bethanyatazadeh@yahoo.com

Cover Design by Stone Ridge Books
Formatting by Bethany Atazadeh
ISBN 10 : 1-7325557-5-3
ISBN 13 : 9781732555754

First Edition: May 2019
10 9 8 7 6 5 4 3 2 1

MARKETING FOR AUTHORS

GROW
YOUR
AUTHOR
PLATFORM

**Generating Book Sales With Your Website,
Email Marketing, Blogging, YouTube & Pinterest
Using Content Marketing**

MANDI LYNN
WITH BETHANY ATAZADEH

CONTENTS

CHAPTER 1:
INTRODUCTION

"A platform is what defines your visibility
with your audience."
—Geraldine Solon

WELCOME TO BOOK two of the *Marketing for Authors Series*! In book one, we talked about the most important part of book marketing: the book itself. If your book isn't polished and set up correctly on Amazon, everything Bethany and I talk about in this book—and in this series as a whole—will be for nothing.

With that said, if you haven't read book one *How Your Book Sells Itself,* make sure you do so before publishing your own book.

There's so much we're going to be talking about in this book! From creating your website and email newsletter, to marketing using your blog, YouTube and Pinterest. We're going to be covering how you can put yourself out there whether you're self-published, traditionally published, or you're still writing the book.

If you want to sell a book, you have to make sure people are aware that you and your book exist.

There are thousands of books being published every day, so you've got competition. You need to stand out and make yourself known. If you're shy, this part will feel terrifying. To which I say, that's a good thing. I'm sure you remember this quote...

Do one thing a day that scares you.

No one has accomplished great things by staying comfortable. You make strides by pushing yourself. So make the world know you wrote a book. Be proud of that. If you haven't published your book yet, be proud that you're writing a book. Do you know how many people say they've always wanted to write a book? I'm sure you've met plenty of random strangers or family members who say they'd like to write a book. You did something they couldn't.

You sat down and started writing.

Be courageous. Be proud of everything you've done.Sit back, invest in yourself, and learn how to make your story heard.

With this book in particular, we're going to talk about how to create and expand your author platform online to make yourself known.

Along the way Bethany and I will be throwing in our own personal experiences of what worked and didn't work for us. Sometimes what works for one person won't work for someone else, and you'll notice that a lot between myself and Bethany. We're both successful in marketing, but sometimes in very different ways. So, take it all in, experiment, and find out what works best for you.

CHAPTER 2:
YOUR AUTHOR WEBSITE

"Websites promote you 24/7:
No employee will do that."
–Paul Cookson

EVERY AUTHOR NEEDS a website. For those who aren't tech savvy, this probably isn't what you wanted to hear. You need a base for your platform, a catch-all for when you meet someone, or they hear about you on social media, and they want to learn more about you.

Social media networks are fads.

They can go away and you have no control over that. In fact, as I'm writing this book, Facebook and Instagram went down for a whole day and everyone was in a panic. *What are we going to do?* But you know who wasn't panicking? Those with a website, because they had their base and a way to access their audience.

On the other spectrum, social media algorithms can change and then suddenly no one is seeing your content. The difference between social media and your website is that you own your website and it's not going anywhere. You have complete control.

If you're the type of author that loves to network online, or go to events and meet people face-to-face, it's so important to have a place you can send people after you've met them—that way you're not just another face. You want people to visit your website and sign up for your newsletter so you'll always be able to keep them as a potential reader.

A website allows you to present yourself as a professional.

You don't need to have a book published to have a website. You just need to have a story to tell. I'm not just talking about the novel you're writing and spending weeks, months, and maybe even years writing, but also the story of your journey as an author. What do you have to tell people? What do you have to offer to the community? Your website is there to showcase your skills, your story, and (once you have a book published) to help you guide people to your Amazon page to buy your book.

Hearing all this may make you groan. Or you may be trying to come up with some theories of your own as to why you *don't* need a website. I promise you, the sooner you start your website and the sooner you begin your email list, the better off you'll be as an author.

Marketing your books starts long before the story is ever published.

Whether you want to be traditionally published or self-published, you'll need to put in some elbow grease to get your book noticed. According to the world's #1 ISBN provider, Bowker, over 1 million books were self-published in 2017, and the numbers only continue to grow each year. And this doesn't even count the number of traditionally published books! There's a lot of competition out there, so why wait until the book is published to start marketing?

A website is a great place to start your marketing platform because it will be the base of everything you do. It's your central hub.

Now, for those who aren't fond of the internet or designing things, you may be cringing, but the good news is that there are many website hosting platforms out there today that make it very easy to have a beautiful website without needing experience in designing a website.

All roads should lead back to your website.

If you have social media profiles, each profile should have a link that leads back to your website in some way, shape or form. The goal of your website is that whenever someone Googles your name, your website is the first thing that comes up. Your website should be the central hub for everything. Just like when someone is on your social media profile and sees a link to your website, when someone goes to your website, they should see links or buttons to all your social media pages and anywhere else you have an online presence. Sound good? Let's get to the technical sides of things for how you're going to create your website.

Give Your Website a Home

Before we start talking about how to create your website, what it will look like and how many pages it will have, let's talk about where it will live on the big-wide-web. Your website's address is its domain.

The domain name is what people will type into their web browser when they come looking for you. It's going to be on your business card and linked on all your social media accounts.

A domain is the URL address of your website. For example: www.authorname.com. A free domain would look like www.wordpress.authorname.com or www.wix.authorname.com.

Purchasing a custom domain to remove your web host's branding is important for many reasons. It makes it easier for someone to remember your domain and it also gives your website authority and professionalism. What do I mean by website authority?

Google ranks custom domains higher than free domains.

This means when someone Googles your name, if you don't have a custom domain, odds are your website won't be one of the top results. On the other hand, if your website does have a custom domain, Google will automatically rank it higher and the odds of it showing up in search results go up significantly.

If you purchase your domain you can name it whatever you'd like, as long as that domain hasn't already been taken. You can host your domain through a variety of websites such as Hostgator, GoDaddy, or FastComet, to name a few. Using these websites, you'll be able to see if your domain has already been taken.

My first recommendation for your domain name is always your first and last name:

www.authorname.com.

If that domain has already been taken, here are a few other examples for ideas:

www.booksname.com

www.nameauthor.com

www.namebooks.com

You get the idea. Anything that has to do with you and what you do. The shorter the better. You want your website to be easy to remember.

Once you purchase your domain, you'll have to sync it to your website host. Wordpress has many tutorials on how to do this and it's usually a pretty simple process. Wix makes the process easy as well—they help walk you through creating a custom domain.

Choosing a Platform to Host Your Website

There are many options to host your website. For all intents and purposes, I'm only going to be talking about website hosts that are known to be very user friendly: Wix and Wordpress. While these are the two hosting platforms I'll be talking about, please know that features I talk about may be available through other hosts as well, so always do your research to find what works best for you!

Between Wordpress and Wix, there are some pretty major differences when it comes to things like ease of use, cost and advanced features. Let's break it down a little.

Blogging

Both website hosting platforms are designed for blogs. Wordpress tends to be the more popular choice when it comes to blogging. But in recent years, Wix has improved their features so more people are leaning toward Wix. If you're interested in learning more about blogging, be sure to read chapter 6. Don't want to blog? While both hosts started out with blogs in mind, you can easily remove the blogging feature off your website.

Designing Your Website Easily

One of the reasons more people are starting to use Wix is because of how user-friendly it is. Editing your Wix website tends to be easier than editing a Wordpress website, because Wix has a drag and drop feature when it comes to designing. You start by choosing a template that you like and then you begin to make your edits from there. It's very easy to customize the look and get things to look exactly how you'd like by adding buttons, pages, and links.

Wordpress also has many capabilities for customization. Similar to Wix, you start by choosing a template or theme, and begin to make your customizations from there. Wordpress can be more difficult for beginners to use, because a lot of the editing of the website is done from the back end and it's less visual than Wix.

If you still feel like you're struggling when it comes to designing your website and figuring out the ins and outs of everything, Bethany and I would love to recommend you to Brittany Wang, a Wix website aficionado, writer, and YouTuber. Brittany works with authors to not only design their Wix website, but also to create a newsletter and get people to sign up for that newsletter. She can teach you how to design your website with her Author Website Bootcamp. If you want her to handle everything for you, she also creates websites or suggests improvements. All-in-all, Brittany is a wealth of knowledge when it comes to Wix websites and newsletters, so her information will be in the back of this book in the resources section if you're interested.

If you're leaning more toward a Wordpress based website, Evie Driver is your go-to girl! Evie is my website designer and she's also a writer and YouTuber. Very soon she'll be starting her website services and resources for authors, so be sure to visit the resources at the back of this book to connect with her as well.

Costs of Your Author Website

Both Wix and Wordpress offer free versions of their websites. While this is great when you're first starting off, I always recommend authors, new or seasoned, to purchase a package/plan so you are able to own your website domain. Purchasing a plan also allows you to remove the Wordpress/Wix branding, as well as ads. This makes your website look more professional.

The prices for Wordpress and Wix can vary on your plan, and your choice of plan will differ depending on what you'd like to do with your website. By the end of this book, you should have an idea of what features you'd like your website to have.

Wordpress Plug-Ins & Features

Wordpress is one of the most popular web hosting websites, and for a good reason. You can do just about anything you'd like with a Wordpress website, but it does come at a cost. In order to get the full effect of Wordpress, you'll need to have their business plan, which will allow you to install plug-ins onto your website.

A basic Wordpress plan will allow you to do just that: the basics. You can edit your website to look however you'd like based off of one of their free templates. Things get a little more advanced if your needs are more complicated. If you want to sell signed copies of your book through your website, you need a plug-in. If you want a form to pop up when someone new visits your website, you need a plug-in. You get the idea. If it's not basic, you need a plug-in.

A plug-in is basically a piece of software that you install into your Wordpress website as an add-on. Each plug-in has a different purpose, and most plug-ins are designed by software developers, so the possibilities of what you can do are endless and there are new plug-ins being created every day. Wordpress is an open-source platform, meaning anyone can go in and edit the HTML code, which allows programmers to create plug-ins to make new features for websites.

Most plug-ins are free, but some come at an additional yearly or monthly cost, or sometimes a one-time fee. Just think of plug-ins as additional features for your website.

Wix Features

Wix is different because you don't need to install plug-ins onto your website. A lot of basic features are in their lowest package, but if you plan on doing anything other than the basics, you'll find yourself somewhat limited in your website's capabilities. Wix is not an open-source platform, meaning the only people making it possible for you to create cool new features for your website is Wix. Wordpress is open-source, meaning anyone can create a new plug-in for their website or write additional code to improve their website.

The good news is Wix has stepped up their game over the years to give you all the necessary bells, and whistles an author may need:

- A shop to sell books

- A pop-up form to get newsletter signups
- Customizable website design templates

If you're not looking for much more than the above, which are the author essentials, then Wix may be for you. If you want complete control without limits, or maybe you want to use your website for something more advanced—like hosting an online course or being able to set up consultation appointments—then Wordpress may be a better choice.

Which website is best for you?

Both website hosts can get pricey depending on what features you're looking for. We'll be talking about some of these features in more detail as we go through this book. My suggestion is to write down or make note of some of the mentioned features as you read. At the end of the book, take your notes and compare them to Wordpress and Wix's pricing plans to see what makes the most sense financially.

You can also get a feel for which website host may be best for you by trying them both out.

You can create both a Wordpress and Wix website for free to test out the waters.

If you find one easier to use than the other, then you can easily purchase a plan and domain for that website.

You can always switch platforms down the line, but the process can be a bit of a headache and confusing if you aren't familiar with how websites are hosted. You need to transfer data such as website pages and blog posts, redirect the domain's name server so your domain knows who your new website host is, and re-design the website's look once all the data has transferred.

All this is possible, but not the easiest thing to do, so try to save yourself time now by doing your research and find a website host that will work for you in the long run.

Mandi's Website:

In case you were wondering, I use Wordpress for my website hosting. I prefer Wordpress because I like to be able to change everything. I have a business plan, so I'm able to download plug-ins, which makes the possibilities for my website endless. I've played around with Wix in the past and almost transferred my website to their hosting, but ultimately my new web designer, Evie Driver, helped me redesign my business and author website in a budget-friendly way and the result was amazing!

Bethany's Website:

Coming from someone who's NOT a fan of using code, the complicated websites felt like knocking my head against the wall in frustration. I gravitated toward Wix as soon as I found out how easy it was to use. The drag-and-drop feature was a huge selling point for me. After testing the website out for a while first, I decided to purchase a plan because of one main reason: they had everything I needed in one place. For someone who doesn't want to spend a lot of time on website creation that was huge! Besides being user-friendly, they have the option to host both your blog and your newsletter directly from their website, plus you can buy your domain name directly through them and skip a third party. Whatever you choose, you will eventually become an expert, but I definitely would recommend Wix to people who are more technologically challenged.

What's on Your Website?

Now that we've gotten the technical side of creating your website out of the way, it's time to talk about some of the pages that your website should have.

Your Must-Have Pages

The following pages and features are things that you should include on your website whether you're a published author or an author to-be.

Social Media Links

This isn't necessarily a page, so much as a set of buttons. Make sure that somewhere on your website there is a list of everywhere you're present on social media. Use the social media icons as buttons, so that if they click it, it will lead them to your social media profile page.

The best-case scenario is to have social media icons that link to your profiles and show up on every page of your website. To do this, the icons would need to be located in the header or footer of your website.

It's All About Me: The Author Bio

Since your website is your home-base for everything, the biography page of your website is probably going to be one of the first pages a new visitor will find if they've just discovered you. Imagine this for a moment: someone discovers you through one of your social media profiles— Instagram for example. Your Instagram bio can only display so much information, but this new potential follower sees that you write young adult fantasy, one of their favorite genres to read! They haven't quite committed to following you, but they visit your website to learn more about you and come across your bio page.

Your bio page is your chance to sell yourself as an author. What else do you do besides writing? Have you published anything? How will following you on social media benefit them? That's the story your website's bio needs to tell.

Need an example of some author bios? Flip to the back of this book and you can read the bios Bethany and I use on our websites, and of course, our books!

Books and/or Work in Progress

The next must-have page on your website is the page for your books. Each book you've written should have its own page. For each published book, you'll need to include the following information:

- Book cover
- Genre
- Blurb
- Link to where people can buy the book

- Link to where people can buy a signed copy of the book (if you sell signed copies)

If you're not published, you can still have a "Books" page on your website. Instead of having information about your published book, give information about your work in progress (WIP). You could share the title, genre, what stage in the process it's in, or any other information that's relevant. If you're unpublished, this page is a great way to convince people that they should follow you so they can stay up to date for the day your book becomes published.

TIPS FROM BETHANY:

I know it can feel awkward to share prior to publishing, but I want to encourage you to create that page for your WIP! You can get people excited for your book long before it's published just by setting up a page and starting to create buzz for the story.

Make sure you don't disclose TOO much information though (such as the whole book for example). The first reason to be cautious about what you share is that you don't want people to steal your ideas. Revealing just enough to pique someone's interest is usually the sweet spot. The second reason is that you also don't want to commit to something, such as a plot twist, the genre, or the world, and then realize after you've revealed it to your audience that you want to change it. My preference is to share details as they become final.

I create a page for each of my upcoming books and/or series and share fun details over time. I like to start by revealing the genre and the subject (for example, an Aladdin-retelling). I have fun using placeholder covers, titles, and imagery (that isn't copyrighted) to spark interest. As time goes on, I like to do a cover reveal and update the website to display the final cover(s) and title(s), as well as a short synopsis of each story, the release dates, a book trailer, and eventually, once the books are released, links to buy them!

Let's Get in Touch:
The Contact Form

This page is easy to set up. The contact page of your website is where you'll have a way for people to email you. Wordpress and Wix make it very easy to set up a contact form so people can send you emails through your website.

Why not just put your email address so people can contact you that way?

Putting your email address up as public information is an option, but you'll notice that if you do that you'll start getting a lot of junk emails. The reason this happens is because there are little website bots that crawl the internet looking for emails. When they find an email on a website, they add it to their list and that's how you get crazy spam from all over the place.

Contact forms were created to prevent this. Forms have an option to prevent bots from reading your email. Have you ever filled out something online and had to click the checkbox to "prove you're human?" Or had to solve a simple math problem or select pictures that are a car? This is the website's way of proving you're not a web bot that will only cause spam or errors.

This is why most people prefer to use a contact form. It's a great way to counteract spam.

On your contact page, you can also include your P.O. Box address, if you have one. Some other fun things you can add to your contact page can be a photo of yourself, links to your social media networks, or anywhere else they can go to get in touch with you!

The Nice-To-Haves

Now that we've talked about all the essential pages of your author website, it's time to talk about the fun pages that aren't necessary but are a great way to connect with your followers.

Getting Offline: The Events Page

An events page is perfect for an author that travels for speaking engagements and book signings. Most authors will use their newsletter to announce when and where they'll be going for events. After you announce the event in your newsletter, you should also add all that information to the events page. This is ideal because you can share the event on social media and use the link to your website as a "home base" for people to visit and learn more.

For your events page, you also have the option of keeping your previous events listed. Having the archive of events is useful to show future venues what you've already done. Your events page can act as a resume of your speaking experience. It can also give your readers an idea of what you've done for events in the past and where you're willing to travel.

On my events page, I put my upcoming events up at the top and as they pass, I move them lower down the page into a separate "past events" section. This isn't necessary, but I love having the archive in case I ever need ideas of events to revisit.

The FAQ Page

The Frequently Asked Questions page can be a fun page to let your readers know more about you than just what's in your bio or on social media. If you often have people asking the same questions over and over, add them to the FAQ page can save you, and them, a little time. When I first became published, a lot of people would ask what it was like to be published as a teen, so you'll see most of my FAQ's are related to that.

You may also get a lot of questions about how to write a book. My suggestion is if you have content (blog posts, videos, posts on social media), instead of answering the questions directly on the FAQ page, you could link over to the content where you answered the question. We'll talk more about your content creation throughout this book, but for now let's move on to the second most important part of your online presence: your newsletter!

CHAPTER 3:
YOUR EMAIL LIST

*"You can't expect to just write and have visitors come to
you—that's too passive."*
—*Anita Campbell*

NOW THAT YOU'VE created your website, it's
time to start your email list for your newsletter.
Your email list, also called your author newsletter,
is vital to your success as an author.

Why is an email list important?

Your newsletter is the only thing that goes directly into your subscriber's inbox. While you can have thousands of followers on social media, it can be hard to connect with them because algorithms can change. Even worse, some social media websites are only fads, which means you could invest a lot of time and energy into your social media page only for it to eventually go "out of style." Or worse, out of business. Having an email list allows you to have direct access to your followers. You don't have to worry about working around a social media algorithm. Your only challenge is to make the subject line of the email interesting enough to open, which we'll talk about soon. But first, let's get your email list set up!

Setting Up Your Email List

There are a few different options when it comes to choosing the platform to host your email list. If you have a Wix website, you can host your email directly through Wix, but it does have some limitations. With Wix's free email marketing feature, you can only send a maximum of three emails a month and you can't have more then 5,000 subscribers before you're required to upgrade to their paid email marketing feature. But just because you have a Wix website doesn't mean you have to use them for your email marketing. You can integrate Wix to most email marketing platforms such as...

- MailChimp
- Constant Contact
- Hubspot
- Convert Kit

MailChimp tends to be the most popular choice for those just starting their email lists because it's free until you reach 2,000 subscribers, and even after that the pricing is modest in comparison to other email hosting websites. While it has some limitations, MailChimp will allow you to do almost anything you may need as an author.

One frustration that authors encounter is that MailChimp requires that you put your address at the bottom of every email you send. I put my P.O. Box address to maintain my privacy, but if you don't have a P.O. Box and don't have any plans to get one, this can be frustrating.

How to Get Email Subscribers

Your newsletter is your #1 marketing tool as an author, since it gives you direct access to your subscribers. However it can be one of the hardest places to grow. It doesn't have a newsfeed or hashtags where people can discover you, and it doesn't show up in search. Your newsletter is just that: a newsletter. So how do you get people to subscribe to it? Well, tell them about it!

Many authors struggle to grow their email list because they don't tell their followers they have one.

Putting a link to your email list on your website is not enough to get people to subscribe.

People want to know that if they're subscribing

to your newsletter, they'll be getting valuable content.

You will have some people subscribe to your email list just because they like you as an author and want to know what you're up to, but most people need an incentive to subscribe. This is where opt-ins come into play.

What is an opt-in?

An opt-in is something you give to your followers in return for them subscribing to your newsletter. It can be as simple as a free one-page printable, or as complex as a link to a one-hour workshop.

Opt-ins work because people like free stuff.

People are very willing to sign up for email lists in return for an opt-in, because even if the opt-in isn't great, they don't lose anything. But if the opt-in is good and they view it as valuable content, they will not only look forward to when you send your next newsletter, but they'll be more willing to pay for content from you in the future. Because if your free content is valuable, imagine how good the paid content is.

What Should My Opt-in Be?

There is an endless number of opt-ins that you can do for your email newsletter. Here are some examples to get your creative juices flowing:

- One or two chapter excerpt of your latest novel
- Habit tracker printable
- In-depth how-to guides
- Templates
- Webinar/workshop
- Cheat sheets/lists
- Exclusive video
- Free ebook
- Character art
- A map of your book's world
- Extra scenes not included in the book (especially if the book is already published)

Start off with at least one email opt-in to get you started. Once you feel more comfortable and you've gotten the hang of things, you can slowly add in more options. The more opt-ins you have, the more subscribers you'll get. The reason you want a few different opt-ins, is that different opt-ins will appeal to different people. Someone may love your webinar, while someone else may prefer your printable template. The more variety of opt-ins you have, the more you'll attract people to sign up for your email list.

Once you've created your opt-in, be sure to tell people about it. Just like with anything else, no one will know about your great opt-in if you don't talk about it on your blog or social media.

How to Set Up Your Email Opt-in

The way you set up your opt-in will vary depending on your email host. The basic premise is to make sure you have a form people can fill out to sign up for your newsletter. You'll want to set it up so that, after they sign up, they'll get a confirmation email. In that email, you'll include a link to whatever opt-in you've created. As I write this book, I have four opt-ins, so I link my subscribers to an unlisted page on my website. This unlisted page is my Resource Library. I have printables, as well as webinar recordings that my subscribers can watch at any time. To see what I mean, you'll just have to subscribe to my newsletter here:

http://bit.ly/MandisNews

Bethany's Newsletter and Opt-Ins

I had a Members Page for a long time as well! Eventually I was giving away so many freebies that I decided to use them for my Patreon page instead, making them exclusive gifts for my patrons over at www.patreon.com/bethanyatazadeh.

However, I made sure to leave two of my favorite opt-ins behind: the first few chapters of my book Evalene's Number *as a gift to subscribers who love to read, plus a Publishing Plan Template with a 23-page guide to planning your novel all the way from the first draft to the release date, as a gift to subscribers who love to write.*

If you're curious, you can subscribe to my newsletter here:

www.bethanyatazadeh.com/contact

How Often to Email

Like I stated earlier in this chapter, you usually want to email at least once a month, as well as whenever there is exciting news. If things are a little slow in the news department, there's nothing wrong with emailing only once a month since we all get so many emails anyways.

Frequency of emails is important. You want to email enough to make sure people remember who you are, but not so much that people begin to unsubscribe from your newsletters. You want your newsletter to be valuable, so that each time someone clicks to read it, it will be exciting information.

Email Pop-Ups

Another trick of the trade is having an email pop-up on your website. This is a cool feature that helps you gain subscribers without having to give it much effort at all. You've probably encountered a pop-up on other websites before. It's a little box that pops up on your screen when you visit a website. If the creator of the newsletter has an opt-in, the pop-up will mention the opt-in. For example:

Want to learn how to design your dream website? Enter your email below to get our free guide.

Sound familiar?

People love free stuff. Having the word free on that little pop-up is gold. If someone was just mildly interested in your website and then a pop-up comes up offering to give them a free guide or something similar, the odds of them subscribing goes up immensely.

You can create a pop-up easily through Wix and Wordpress. To create one on Wordpress, however, you will need a business plan and to download one of the many plug-ins they offer to create pop-ups.

Once you start creating your pop-up, try to make it attractive and to match the branding of the rest of your website. Make it so the "X" out button is easily visible. If you hide the button to close the pop-up you'll annoy people and they'll leave your website entirely.

An important setting of a pop-up is setting up cookies. In this case, a cookie basically tells your website how long it's been since someone's been on your website. You can adjust your website's cookies to make it so the pop-up will only come up if someone hasn't been to your website in a selected amount of days or months. Let's say you set it for 30 days. Someone comes to your website. The pop-up comes up and they either close the pop-up or fill it out. They can now visit the website every day for 30 days without the pop-up coming up again.

Why is this important? Well, imagine being someone who visits a website and no matter what, every single time this annoying pop-up comes up on their screen. If it gets really annoying, they may stop visiting the website altogether.

When it comes to adjusting the settings of your pop-up, you want to be somewhere between popping up enough so that people won't miss it, but not so often that you start to annoy people.

Writing Your Subject Line

Since the subject line of your email is what determines whether or not someone will open the email, let's dive deeper into creating a catching email subject! Writing a good subject line comes with practice. I'll admit, it's something I still haven't mastered, but I do notice I'm getting better.

Think of the emails you get on a daily basis. Which ones do you open and why? Odds are it's something in the subject line that sounds interesting or is timely. Having a subject line that's timely is huge. This could mean the email is referencing something going on right now (an event or holiday) or you phrase the email title in a way that shows your subscribers the contents of the email are only meanful if you open it *right now* (a sale or special offer). People have access to emails on their phones now. They know when they receive an email almost instantly, and the email subject line is visible. Your email subject line determines whether someone will ignore the notification and forget about the email or open the email right away.

41

Try to think flashy when it comes to writing the subject line of your email. The term "click bait" comes to mind. You want to hook someone into reading your email, but you don't want to make false promises.

Create a sense of urgency to make someone want to open the email right away, or hint at the content the email contains.

Also think short and sweet, because you've only got so many words to work with before they're cut off! Your email subject should be no longer than 40-60 characters, maximum. Avoid using words like "free" and "earn money" or anything of the like, because often times your email will end up in the spam folder.

Here are some tips when it comes to writing your email subjects:

- Get right to the point of what your email is all about
- Create a sense of urgency
- Make it funny, interesting or exciting
- Give it a shock value
- Show what you have to offer

Again, you'll get better with your subject lines with practice. If you're an author that does monthly newsletters, don't have the email subject be "June Newsletter" or something of the like. If you're a big fan of that author, you'll probably open it, but if you're not then the email sounds boring and you may not even open it. Give people a reason to open your newsletter and see what you have to say.

What to Write in Your Newsletter

Nine times out of ten, you'll be using your newsletter as a tool to update your followers on what you've been up to. Here are some ideas of what to include in your newsletter:

- Events you'll be attending
- Sales that are going on

- Exciting events happening on social media (Twitter chats, YouTube livestreams, Instagram photo challenges, etc.)
- Collaborations you're doing with other authors or companies
- Your latest blog, vlog, feature, or guest post

You can also use your newsletter to remind readers to write reviews of your book on Amazon and Goodreads. Reviews are vital to authors when it comes to making a sale with other potential readers. While we, the authors, know this, someone who reads a book for the sake of reading a book doesn't know just how important a review can be. Most of the time, people are more than happy to write a short review, they just don't know how much it matters or they forget. Try to remind readers to write a review every now and then. Don't put the reminder in every newsletter though, because after a while people will stop seeing it—or even worse, get annoyed and unsubscribe.

If you haven't sold many books in a while, remind people to write a review or share with their friends or even just talk about why they liked the book. There's so much you can do to help you get more reviews, but we'll talk about that more later on in this series.

What to put in emails

There's so many different things you can put in your newsletter. Promo for other authors, special promotions when you're launching a book, a product or service, and so on. The options for your newsletters are endless, but if you need some ideas, I've broken things down into two different stages of your author career:

Stage 1: Not-Yet-Published and Don't Have Much Under Your Belt

It's never too early to start marketing your book, even if it's not finished or not published yet. Most people won't care whether or not you've published anything. If you deliver good content, they'll stick around.

Talk About Your Journey: In your newsletter you can talk about how the writing process is going and try to make it exciting and unique to you. It's not uncommon for your readers to also be writers. They know how tedious the writing process is and how it can also be as boring as staring at a wall, thinking about how to write the next chapter. And even if those subscribed to your newsletter aren't writers and they just love to read, they'd love to hear progress as you come closer to publishing your book. It's an exciting process and they want to be the first ones to know when the book is done!

If you're going to use your newsletter to talk about yourself, use your skill as a writer to make what feels like a "boring life" sound interesting. Make your subscribers fall in love with the writing in your newsletter so they'll want to see your writing in a book someday.

What You've Learned: As a writer, you can never learn enough. Each writer has a different way they go about the craft, so share your way. Educate your subscribers and try to make your newsletter something they look forward to each time it's in their inbox. There's no wrong way to write, so talk about it openly.

Updates: This is similar to talking about your journey, but it's more specifically about updating your subscribers on your progress. Share milestones with them. Have you finished writing the first draft of your novel? Celebrate! Did you query your first agent? Tell them all about it. Share your ups and downs in your author career, because we all have them. The more genuine you are, the more people will support you in your career.

I didn't start my email newsletter until 2018, which I regret because I've missed so many opportunities to easily grow my list. While I can't attest to having a newsletter before I was published, I did have a YouTube channel before I was published. On my channel I talked about how to write books and how I was publishing my novel. I taught people something valuable, while also talking about my book, which meant as the day approached for its publication, everyone was excited.

And guess what? People *do* care about your journey.

You don't want to make it *all* about you, but you want to make yourself relatable. Frame your newsletters and content in a way that someone will see it and want to click on it because:

1. They want to learn
2. They'll relate to whatever you're saying

A great example is if you talk about self-doubt. Every writer faces this, so when another author talks about it, people react and engage with your content because they don't feel so alone anymore. But please know that if you are talking about something negative like self-doubt and writer's block, it's helpful to end on a positive note. No one likes a Debbie Downer. People want a pep talk! Not for you to confirm their worst fears.

Stage 2: Published (or About to Be) and Ready to Fly

48

This is when sending your newsletter becomes really important because you either have a book that you're almost ready to market, or your book is already out in the world looking for reader. You can do any of the ideas mentioned in stage one, but as someone further along in their career, you might have a few more things up your sleeve.

Content Updates: If you have a blog, YouTube channel, podcast, ad other content, you can use your newsletter to do a summary of all the content that you've created that month. Try highlighting your favorite piece of content and telling your subscribers why it's important for them to check it out.

Book Updates: As you're getting ready to publish a book, you'll start to notice that there will be a lot of updates. So many that you won't be able to fit it all into one newsletter. These are the cases when you're going to have to send out more frequent emails then your usual once-a-month emails. You'll want to send out a separate email each time you reveal one of the following:

49

- Publication date
- Cover reveal
- Pre-order annoucements
- Book trailer
- Blog tour
- Events
- Any campaigns or sales related to the book release

You don't have to choose just one thing to talk about in your newsletter. You can mix it up every now and then, or you can try to do a little bit of everything. I encourage you to do the latter.

Don't be afraid to try new things.

If you experiment, try to keep an eye on the open rate and unsubscribe rate of your emails. If you're noticing people aren't opening the emails as much anymore, or if people have started to unsubscribe, try to look back at what you've been doing differently to connect the dots as to why they aren't enjoying your content as much as they had been. Are the email titles no longer drawing people in? Is the content less interesting or helpful? Are you emailing too often? There's always a reason why something is or isn't working, so discover that reason and fix it.

TIPS FROM BETHANY:

Perfectionism can be a huge stumbling block for people when it comes to newsletters. "What if I don't get it right? What if it's not interesting? What do I even say?"

I just want to reiterate what Mandi said: just start. It's better to make mistakes now when you have a few loyal subscribers who will understand, then if you leave the learning curve for later when a larger audience might see it. Trust me.

It's also truly the most valuable thing you can do for book sales, because having the ability to tell even just a small but loyal group of people about your book on release day could make a massive difference in your author career. It could get you on a best sellers list! It could double your sales! It could encourage those people to tell their friends and spread the word.

All of these things are possible with social media, but the difference is:

1) you're reaching people who went out of their way to sign up for this information and are therefore your warmest leads, and,

2) there aren't any algorithms getting in your way!

So, push through the nerves and the what ifs, and just go for it!

CHAPTER 4:
CONTENT
MARKETING

"Content is anything that adds value to the reader's life."
—*Avinash Kaushik*

CONTENT MARKETING! WHAT is it and what's the point of it?

To put it simply, content marketing is when you create valuable and helpful content that is distributed to a clearly defined audience, which ultimately leads to a profitable action.

Let's take blogs for example. You're writing a blog about working out. You're teaching people to do different stretches and simple workouts. It becomes marketing when, at the end of some of your blog posts, you mention that if they'd like to take things a step further, they can sign up for some of the paid, virtual classes.

The essence of content marketing is establishing trust with your audience.

You offer free content to show people you know what you're talking about.

Unfortunately, this theory doesn't always translate well for authors. Odds are, the free content you create won't directly translate to what your book is about. For example, I create videos on YouTube about marketing, self-publishing, and writing. If I wrote books on these subjects, that would be great. But this book is the first time I've written non-fiction. Up until this point I've only ever written novels. So, things shift a little bit for authors when it comes to content marketing. For fiction authors, content marketing is different because you're not always creating content to help sell your book directly, you're often creating content to make yourself known. The more content you create, the more people you reach. The more people you reach, the more potential readers you gain.

It's not impossible to use content marketing to directly sell your books, but the process tends to be simpler. Instead of offering knowledge as content, you're offering bits of the book. Share your favorite quotes or take pictures of the book and post them on Instagram. Get creative to bring attention to your book!

Getting Discovered

For authors, content marketing is still about gaining trust, but it is also about figuring out how to get people to know you exist in the first place. You do this by creating valuable content that people are looking for. When you do this, people will come to you naturally. You need to create a name for yourself and a *platform*. That way, when the book is published, you have a following of people you can tell about it. Because you've created valuable content, people will think, "They created this great blog post about writing a book! So their book must be great!" And they'll buy your book.

You want people to follow you, not just because you wrote a book, but because you offer great content. The more content you produce, the more memoriable you become. They'll follow you for great content you create, and this includes the books you publish. Being an author is hard because it can take months or even years to write and publish a book. Your readers might forget you in that time, but if they follow you online and you're posting videos or writing a blog, they'll remember you.

Answer the question
people are asking

How do you create that great content? You may be thinking, I can write a blog about myself! Or, I can write book reviews! Or, I can just talk about books! For some people, that works, but it's often left up to chance as to whether the content you create will catch on.

The best way to gain a following online is by answering people's most frequently asked questions. When I was writing my debut novel, there weren't many videos on YouTube about writing and self-publishing. As I was figuring out how to do things myself, I began making videos about the process on my YouTube channel. When I learned how to format my novel, I made a video on formatting. When I made a book trailer for my novel, I made a video about that too. I had all these questions when I self-published my first book, so once I found the answer, I made a video and put it on YouTube.

By the time my first book came out, I had more than a thousand people following me, ready to buy my book. Did every one of my followers buy my book? No. And I wouldn't expect them to. Not all my followers read young adult fantasy. But the ones that did bought the book.

My following on YouTube began to climb, because I was answering the questions that everyone was asking. When you're trying to figure out what type of content to create, think about what people always have questions about and work from there.

This isn't limited to just how-to videos.

Try to think outside of the box. For example, if you write fantasy or sci-fi, odds are your readers are also into sci-fi and fantasy movies. For those types of fans, you can connect with them and find them by creating content specific to that genre. This could mean a blog post about the best Comic Cons, or tips to create a great cosplay outfit, and things of the like. Get in the head of your reader and discover what their interests are. What types of things are they looking up on the internet? That's the content you should create.

Create Something Worth Sharing

Everyone wants to go viral. But being viral does not mean lifelong success. Viral is a trend, and just like everything else, it comes and goes, so don't shoot for something to go viral. Be a constant source of shareable content. Have you ever watched a video and immediately wanted to share it? That's shareable content. The creator didn't ask you to share the content. The content itself did all the heavy lifting. Next time you come across a piece of content that you immediately wanted to share with someone, ask yourself: what was it that made you react that way?

Sharable content sparks
an emotion.

Give your viewers a reason to laugh, to cry, to feel hope. Writing is a lonely activity. The process can feel draining at times, so tell your story. Open up and talk about your dreams and fears about being a writer and you'll find that your journey gets less lonely. Make a connection with your audience and start a conversation.

Here are some things you can do to make your content shareable:

- Tell a story
- Validate an opinion
- Appeal to values & experiences
- Be useful
- Make your information easy to digest
- Join trends
- Inspire people
- Make people laugh

Create the Superfan

The best part about content marketing is the idea that you create a superfan. When you create content. I don't want you to just write a blog post, post about it, and forget it. You need to interact with the community. When you interact with the community, you create a superfan.

To explain what a superfan is, I want to you step into the mind of a reader. Imagine you just finished reading a book. It wasn't anything special, but you liked it enough to give it a four-star rating. You post a picture of it on your Instagram and tag the author. Maybe you do this all the time, but the authors never notice. But not this time. This time when you posted the picture, the author not only liked the photo, but commented on it. Wow! As a reader, this feels pretty cool! The author noticed you! This four-star book that you would have put back on the shelf and forgot about now just became a little more relevant in your life! The author knows who you are! If you're a little bit of a book nerd, you may tell your friends. This book is no longer forgettable because the author made an effort to connect with you.

As an author, I want you to connect with your audience. I want you to re-create an experience like this. Interact with your audience not only in the content you create online, but also when you see people reading your book. Comment and say thank you. Ask them if they had a favorite scene. Start a conversation with them so you become memorable. Not only so they tell people about your book, although that's a bonus. You want to create a connection with them because maybe they'll read your next book too. As an author, you're nothing without your readers, so show them they're valuable to you.

Create a Connection

When you're an author and a content creator you get to connect with your following in ways that most authors never do. Your followers come to expect your weekly blog posts or videos. They feel like they know you on a more personal level than if they just read your book.

Your followers shift from being typical readers to superfans.

People begin to feel like they're friends with you, and this is another reason why they buy your book. I've had people buy my book, knowing they don't usually like that genre, but they buy it because they want to support me and my career.

I think of it like this: When you publish a book, your friends and family buy the book because they want to support you. They tell their friends and coworkers about it because they're proud of you. Essentially, you're creating this same sort of connection with your followers. Not quite to that extent, but it's similar.

The type of support you feel when you create a platform for yourself using content marketing is unbelievable. Book sales aside, having an online following helps pick you up when you're down. Your followers are there to help you through this sometimes stressful journey of being an author. Odds are, even if it doesn't help you sell a book, they'll give you a confidence boost.

That's why you need
to content market

Now that you know why it works and how it works, I hope you go into the next few chapters full of ideas and excitement!

CHAPTER 5:
SEARCH ENGINE OPTIMIZATION

"Google only loves you when everyone else loves you

first."

—Wendy Piersall

BEFORE WE DIVE into creating specific types of content, I want to talk a little bit about SEO, which stands for search engine optimization. How you optimize your content is how you can affect the way

Google sees your content and decides how it will rank in search engine results. The better your SEO, the more likely your content will be seen.

The Magic of Keywords

Keywords are the way you help search engines find your content. Keywords are, more or less, hot topics, words, or phrases. They're things people search a lot, so you want to make sure you include them in your content so the search engine can pick them up.

An example of some writing-related keywords are...

- Writing
- Writing advice
- Writing tips
- How to write a book
- How to write a book in a month

A keyword is a word or phrase that's commonly searched and will help index your content on search engines.

And by index, I literally mean catalog and file into a specific category. Let's visualize this for a moment. Google has little bots, and those bots roam through the world wide web and comb through every blog post, image, video and so on. The bots are searching for keywords and they organize content according to keywords, as well as many other factors.

When someone goes on Google and searches "how to write a book," Google takes an index it created and organizes the search results within that index, according to different factors, such as use of keywords, clicks on the website, and so much more.

Google is constantly changing their algorithm to improve search results, so the goal isn't to learn the algorithm, but to create engaging content.

Because that's all search engines are really after! They're optimized for the user, so above all, create your content with the user in mind.

Keywords are for more than just Google. Keywords affect how you show up on YouTube, Pinterest, social media, Amazon and everywhere else on the internet. And yes, keywords affect how your book shows up when people are searching for books on Amazon, but if you read book one in this series, you already knew that, right?

Finding Keywords That Work For You

Finding good keywords is easier said than done. Sometimes it can be hard to find good keywords to include in your content. One of my favorite tools to use is a plug-in for your desktop. If you download the plug-in, Keywords Everywhere, you'll be able to search anything in Google and in the right-hand bar there is a list of other common phrases or words people search.

For example, if I know I'm making a blog post or video about self-publishing a novel, I can search "self-publishing a novel" and these are some of the suggestions it gives me:

- How to publish a book for free
- How much does it cost to self-publish a book
- How to self-publish a book on Amazon
- Best self-publishing companies
- Free self-publishing
- Steps to self-publish a book
- Easiest way to publish a book

These are all the results the plug-in gives me, so it allows me to know what exactly people are searching for. I can pick and choose which ones are relevant to my blog post/video and make sure it's included in the content so it's searchable; or if they aren't relevant to my topic exactly, I can write these down to use as topics to cover later on.

Keywords are the Hashtags of Google

If you're still having trouble understanding what keywords are, think of them like hashtags. Social media uses hashtags to help you discover things on social networks, but keywords help you discover things online in general.

If you search #writing on Twitter or Instagram, the results will be too general and probably not what you're looking for, but it you search #5amwritersclub, you'll get results from everyone who wakes up at 5 am to write and uses this hashtag. Just like hashtags, the more specific you get with keywords, the more likely you are to find what you're looking for. Or if you're a content creator, the more likely that you'll be discovered by the people actually looking for the content that you create.

Keywords Are Not Tags

Keywords are not the same as tags or hashtags, which is what you add to your blog or YouTube videos. You should always use your keywords as tags, but you also want to use your keywords everywhere you can, such as in your blog post and blog title. In a video, you want to use your keywords in your video description and video title. On your website, you'll have keywords as well that can help people find your content when searching on google. When you have keywords, try to use them as much as possible without going overboard. If you use too many of the same keyword, the content gets flagged and pushed lower down in the algorithm.

TIPS FROM BETHANY:

I like to think of keywords as my little library reference cards. If the internet is the "library" where everyone is searching for all kinds of things, then the library reference cards (AKA keywords) tell them where to find you and/or your work. Even your name is a keyword. Your books are keywords. Your blog titles and website name are keywords.

You're constantly using keywords when you put out content, whether you realize it or not.

But you have the opportunity when you choose these keywords to either choose at random and hope they work, or be intentional and make the most of them.

Choosing the latter, and putting time into figuring out the best keywords for that particular content, can make a HUGE difference.

To use the analogy above, it's the difference between choosing a "library reference card" that no one wants and no one is searching for, or choosing one that sends a ton of traffic your way. That's the power of keywords!

CHAPTER 6:
BLOGGING

"Marketing is really just about sharing your passion."
—*Michael Hyatt*

TO BLOG OR not to blog, that is the question!

A blog is not necessary for your author platform, but it can help you build your following if you do it correctly. If you have a blog on your website, make the blog feed the home page/landing page of your website, so when someone visits, that's the first thing they see.

While a blog can be the entirety of a website, I mention it last because, as an author, it is not at all necessary to have. If you decide to have a blog on your website, read on! If you've tried a blog and it never seemed to catch on, I suggest you read this chapter for some tips and tricks that may help you.

If you create content in some other form (a YouTube channel, a podcast, etc.) you can repurpose this material for your blog. For example, if you have a YouTube channel, you can post your newest YouTube video with a short description of what your video is about. The short description of your video is helps add keywords to your blog post and improve SEO. Or you can post the YouTube video along with a written out "blog" version that repeats what is covered in that video.

Blog Topics

"How to" blog posts are great ways to build your author platform. They perform well in Google's search engine because these are topics and questions people want answered. While it may be tempting to do a blog post documenting your journey as an author, you'll find you'll have a hard time growing a following because that's not what people are searching for. You'll find a few followers, but if your blog has a focus on how-to topics, it will grow exponentially.

Here are some ideas for topics for your blog:

- How to write a book
- How to self-publish a book
- How to traditionally publish a book
- How to market/sell your book
- How to build your author platform
- How to stay motivated

These are broad topics that you can then branch off into smaller, more specific topics.

Think Twice Before Reviewing Books

Besides using a blog to document your journey as an author, or to post how-to articles, or tips and tricks, another option people use their blogs for is to write book reviews. This is an extremely popular option, but as an author it's an option I try to sway writers away from.

As a reader, it makes sense to write book reviews on your blog. After all, writing book reviews is the #1 way of supporting an author. However, if you're an author yourself, writing book reviews can get a little sticky.

When you're a reader and you come across a book you don't like, it's easy enough to write a quick review on Goodreads or Amazon saying why you didn't enjoy the book. You know you'll never meet the author, so things won't get awkward. When you're an author, things are different. The odds of meeting another author, even one that you think you'll never cross paths with (online or offline), are much higher. Authors do read reviews of their books, so try to imagine if you wrote a bad review of a book and eventually you went on to meet that author. Writing bad book reviews can burn bridges before they're even formed.

At the end of the day, nothing is stopping you from doing a blog on book reviews, but my recommendation is to avoid publicly giving reviews unless you're providing quotes for a book for marketing purposes and/or highly recommend the book.

How to Write a Good Blog Post

Now that you have an idea of what topics you'd like to cover for your blog, it's time to talk about how you should write your blog. For this section, I want you to think about some blogs you've read in the past and how those blog posts were written. Most popular blogs follow a similar format:

- A lot of headers
- Paragraphs with clear direction
- Bullet points

It's a simple formula, but an effective one.

People can be lazy, especially when reading blog posts. There's so much content on the internet that people tend to skip things, and the same goes for blog posts. If someone stumbles across a blog post, they'll skim it to see if it's useful before they start reading it word for word. People will skim the headings to see if it covers the desired topics.

If the headings are interesting, they're more likely to read the entire blog post. The headings also help with search engine optimization (SEO). Google and other search engines treat headings differently; they treat the words in headings as more important than the words in the paragraphs. If you put keywords in your headings, your SEO ranking will be that much better.

Is It a Header or a Style?

Here's a quick web coding and web design lesson to help you optimize your website. H stands for heading. Your H1 (Header 1) is your blog post title. If you've made blog posts before, I'm sure you've seen the style choices of having your text be an H1, H2, H3 and so on. The point of these "styles" is not to make your text pretty, it's so you can tell Google what is the most important text. I'm telling you this because some websites, like Wordpress, let you choose what type of headers you want, but most users see it as a style choice, rather than an option to optimize their website.

Your blog post needs to have a few different things to be SEO friendly:

- An H1 (Heading 1/Main Header)
- A handful of H2's (Header 2/Sub-Headers)

You should only have one H1 for your blog post, and that H1 is your post's title. Your H2's are the titles of the sections within the blog post. You can have a handful of H2's. Throw a few keywords into your headings and your blog is now search engine friendly!

Using headings and breaking things up with multiple paragraphs and bullet points are also great for your readers. Like I said, people like to skim. If the paragraphs are too dense, they might not read the blog post. To see what I mean, look at blogs with a new set of eyes and notice how they are formatted. Do you see the headings? The short paragraphs? The bullet points? This is all to make reading easier and to improve the SEO of the blog post. You'll also notice that this book series is written in a similar style because it is easier to read.

Call to action

With every blog post you write, you should have a call to action. You've just provided valuable information in your blog post and now it's time to wrap things up, but before you do, ask the readers for something in return. Remind them to subscribe to the blog, or ask them a question so they can answer it in the comments. Your goal is to get engagement. If they liked the blog, they'll subscribe so they can see more. If you asked a question and they answer it in the comments, that improves your search ranking. If you have another blog post on a similar subject, lead them to that other blog post.

You always want to keep people engaged.

Try to do whatever you can to get people to stay on your website. The longer someone stays on your website and the more pages they visit, the better Google ranks you in search results.

Each time someone reads a blog post by you, they see you as a leader in the industry. When you establish trust with someone like this, the odds of them buying your book and supporting you as an author grow tremendously.

How Often to Post

The amount of times you should post on your blog varies, but a good rule of thumb is a least once a week. Most people actually suggest posting on your blog at least two or three times a week, but as long as you create content at least once a week and it's good, quality content, that should be appropriate. Always think: quality over quantity.

Get Visual With Imagery

Every blog post you create should have an image to accompany it. This is not only because it helps with SEO, but also because people are visual. We like reading blog posts, but we also enjoy the image that goes along with it.

The image you create gives you something to share on social media to help lead people to your blog as well. The post's image should be something relatively simple that includes the blog post's title. Even better is if it's designed with Pinterest in mind, because Pinterest can be the #1 way to grow your blog, but we'll talk about that more in later chapters!

SEO for Your Blog Post

Let's talk search engine optimization. Like I said in a previous chapter, keywords are what will help your content show up on search engines. For each blog post, you'll want to have one or two main keywords. These main keywords should be in everything. This means the blog title, the post itself (a couple of time probably), and in tags. After the main keywords, you'll have many other keywords that branch off from there. These are usually the long-tail keywords, which are keywords that are usually at least four words long, sometimes more. Try to throw these keywords into the blog post itself if you can, but at the very least try to include them all in the tags of the blog post.

How to grow your blog following:

There are so many different ways you can grow your blog's following. Some ways are direct, while other are indirect. Here are my top favorite ways to grow your blog following:

1. Comment and follow other blogs

It's hard to grow your blog following, because it's a standalone website. The best way to get other people to find you is by putting yourself out there and commenting on other blog posts. This is also a great way to network and connect with other bloggers.

2. Guest post on other blogs

If you've found you love a blog and you've connected a lot with the creator of the blog, ask if you can do a guest post and if they'd also like to do a guest post on your blog. This makes it a win-win for both of you.

3. Encourage people to share your blog post

This one is simple. At the end of your blog post, simply mention that if they liked the post, that they should share it online or tell their other writerly/book nerd friends about it! You can't believe how willing people are to share something if you just remind them to!

4. Share your blog post on other platforms

Don't let other parts of your author platform go to waste. Share your blog to your social media sites to help drive traffic to the post. Just because someone follows you on Twitter or Instagram doesn't mean they also follow your blog, so tell them about the latest posts!

Mandi's Blog

My blog is a little different from most blogs. Because my focus is my YouTube channel, I use my blog as a feed for my videos. Each time I have a new video, I post it as a blog post and add the embedded video in, along with a description. This way I have another place to share my video, and it's still SEO optimized as a blog post because it has all the keywords that make it show up in search.

I used to write a blog post version for all my YouTube videos. I did this because I wanted a proper blog. I ultimately stopped doing a full blog post because it took so much time, when I wanted my time to be spent on my YouTube channel. I'm not a blogger. I'm a YouTuber. For me, there was no point in writing up full blog posts if I wasn't passioniate about it. Instead, I repurpose my YouTube videos. I already have the content, so I post the videos as blog posts and reap the rewards. If I ever have time to fully invest in my blog in the future, I might go back to writing full blog posts for each video, but until then, I let the video speak for itself.

TIPS FROM BETHANY:

I originally started out with a blog as well, and now have switched my time to a YouTube channel (which we'll talk about in the next chapter). But the truth is that both of these these types of content creation take up a LOT of time. I'm talking vast quantities of time that you could be using to write.

So, if you choose to pursue either of these avenues, I always suggest making sure you actually enjoy them.

For example, while I love writing long, rambling Instagram posts, when it came to a blog, the content creation suddenly felt like this overwhelming chore that I didn't enjoy at all. I paid attention to that. I asked myself why I was pursuing something I didn't enjoy, and I stopped. Maybe someday I'll decide to repurpose my Instagram posts into blog posts as well, turning that work into extra content.

It all comes down to is this: there's no right or wrong time to start a blog. And there's no requirement that an author has to do a blog either. But if you do decide to take this step, I would suggest a trial period to make sure it's a good fit and then, if you do decide it's the right fit for you, commit to it fully and show up consistently.

CHAPTER 7:
YOUTUBE

*"You can never go wrong by investing in communities
and the human beings within them."*
—Pam Moore

IT'S NOW TIME to talk about something that most authors don't think about when it comes to creating a platform for themselves: YouTube. YouTube has become my favorite platform over the years, and while part of it is because I've been on YouTube since 2012, the other part is just because I love the platform as a whole for connecting with my audience.

A Little Bit of History

If you don't use YouTube much yourself, you may be surprised when I tell you there a ton of authors on YouTube. You may also be surprised when I tell you that there's a name for this community: AuthorTube. I'll give you some unofficial back history first…

As of 2019, the term AuthorTube is still relatively new. Before AuthorTube, there was BookTube, which was people reading and talking about books. Videos in the BookTube community included book hauls, book reviews, tags and anything book related. The BookTube community quickly grew and some creators grew to have thousands of followers. Enough for the publishing companies to take notice. Publishers would send BookTubers books for free in exchange for featuring those books on their channels. BookTubers also began attending book events like

BookCon and were featured in the same way New York Times Best-Selling authors would be featured. This proves how powerful YouTube can be as a marketing tool.

AuthorTube

AuthorTube eventually became a branch off of BookTube. People, like myself, were interacting with the BookTube community, but instead of doing book reviews, we were talking about how to write and publish a book. More and more people started doing videos like this until one day, the term AuthorTube became a part of the community. Authors or future authors were creating videos, making a connection with their followers, and networking with other authors to build their audiences and publish their books.

What do authors talk about?

As you know from the content marketing chapter, the best type of content answers the most popular questions that people ask. When you create videos like that, you're discovered. There's a reason my top video on YouTube is about the costs of self-publishing. It wasn't by chance. It's because the first thing people ask when they consider self-publishing their book is, how much will it cost?

Filming YouTube Videos

Creating YouTube videos isn't as easy as writing a blog post. When you're writing a blog post you can sit on the couch in your pajamas, write something up, and hit publish. Creating a YouTube video is a little more complicated.

To give you an idea of just how complicated, let's look at all the steps I go through when I'm creating a video…

1. Write script
2. Get dressed and look presentable for camera
3. Set up filming lights and camera
4. Record video
5. Download video footage onto my computer
6. Edit the video footage
7. Upload to YouTube

8. Set up the video so it is SEO friendly

9. Hit publish on the video

I'll be honest when I say this is a very simplified version of my process, but you get the idea. I do have a few tricks to make things a little easier though. I tend to film all my videos for the month at once, which means steps 1 through 4, I do all at once and only once a month. Do you have to do each and every one of these steps? No. But there's a reason you should.

Quality Matters

I want you to think to yourself for a minute, how many people you follow on YouTube whose videos have bad lighting or the sound isn't good, or the person on camera looks kind of messy or the background of the video is messy. Probably not many, and there's a reason for that. As a society, we're vain. We're not proud of it, but we are. We like things to be bright, crisp, clean, and well presented. If we watch a video were the lighting is bad or the video isn't well edited, odds are you won't like the video even if that person is presenting valuable information.

So yes, for YouTube videos you have to put more effort into the process, but the outcome is worth it. When you put that much more effort into it, you put yourself one step above all the other thousands of videos on YouTube, which increases your odds of being noticed.

How to Create Quality Videos

What's the secret to a quality video? Good lighting. That's all there is to it. Good lighting can sometimes be the difference between an okay video and a professional looking video.

This doesn't mean you have to go out and spend hundreds of dollars on filming lights. Natural light is the best thing to film in, so just try to film when the sun is up and shining. Choose a spot to film where the background would look nice in the video and has nice lighting during the day, preferably facing the window.

You may also be surprised when I tell you that you don't need an expensive camera. I know plenty of AuthorTubers who get by with filming on their phone or laptop because they have good lighting.

If you'd like recommendations of good filming lights, visit the resources section in the back of this book.

Writing a Script

Before you start filming, try to write a script. As a viewer, there is nothing more frustrating than having to wait 3 minutes to get the quality information because the person is droning on about nothing important or talking themselves in circles. Write yourself a simple script so you cover all your points without going off topic. Some people like writing their script out word for word, but I personally like using bullet points/talking points as my script.

The format of your script should be simple:

- Intro/Hook
- Tips and advice/Delivering on the hook
- Closing and call to action

Introducing Yourself

The intro of your video needs to be short. People are here for the information you're about to provide, not to hear you talk about yourself. For your intro, state who you are, and why you're qualified to talk about the topic on hand. Your intro shouldn't be more than a few sentences. Here's mine:

"Hello everyone! My name is Mandi Lynn. I'm the author of the fantasy novels, *Essence, I am Mercy*, and thriller novel, *She's Not Here*. I'm also the creator of AuthorTube Academy, and today we're going to be talking about _____."

This intro tells people that I'm an experienced author, meaning I know how to write and publish books, and if they're familiar with AuthorTube, they'll probably get curious as to what AuthorTube Academy is. My goal is to give them enough information to know who I am, but if they want to learn more about me, all they have to do is scroll down to the video's description where there are links to everything I mention in my intro.

Hook The Viewer

The hook of my intro is when I say what that video is about. Why should they stick around to watch the video and how will the content be valuable to them? You want to do this in about a sentence or two so you can jump right into the content of the video.

Deliver on the Hook

Just like writing a blog post, your video has a body and that's the tips and advice you're going to deliver. You want your tips to be concise and clear. You can also give your own opinions and personal experiences. If you're giving tips on writing, know that writing is subjective. There's almost always more than one way to do something, whether writing, editing, publishing, or marketing, so remember when you share videos that you're sharing your opinion, not the *only* way. When you create a "how-to" video, you're saying how you personally write, and hopefully your process will help or inspire someone else in their writing journey. If someone does it differently, that does not make them wrong.

Closing Your Video & Call to Action

At the end of your video, sum things up by reminding them what they learned and give them a call to action. Ask them to comment on the video, or subscribe, or maybe visit you on your website. For my videos, I like to ask a question so my viewers can answer the question in the comments. This interaction tells YouTube it was a good video and they'll be more likely to suggest the video to other users. The more comments, likes and views on a video, the better.

I also like to direct people to subscribe to my newsletter and I let them know about all the free downloads they'll get when they do subscribe. I also do marketing consultations and design book covers, so I do a quick mention to make sure my followers know everything I do in case they're every looking for a designer or one-on-one help with marketing.

What If I'm Camera Shy?

I know what you're thinking. This is all great, but what if you don't like being on camera? You don't need to use YouTube as a part of your author platform, but when done correctly it can be a huge help. If you're curious about it, I invite you to try it out for a bit. Everyone is awkward on camera at first. Go to my YouTube channel and watch some of my old videos. They're cringe worthy. Just like everything else, practice makes perfect, so don't dismiss the possibility of YouTube too soon.

But Every Topic Has Already Been Covered

It's true, everyone and their mother has made a video about how to write a book, or how to outline a book, and so on. But everyone has their own process, so talk about *your* process. Find your niche in the AuthorTube community. Make comedy videos, or cover the business of being an author, or marketing a book. You can even cover topics exclusive to a genre.

Personally, my favorite types of videos to both make and watch are pep talks. Being a writer is hard, so make encouraging videos reminding people why they should keep fighting for their dream.

How Often to Post

A best practice is to post on YouTube at least once a week. Consistency is key when it comes to creating any content and it's how you stay visible and relevant. I used to post videos twice a week and it helped me boost my following for a while, but ultimately, I got burnt out and my videos weren't as good. For this reason, I went back to posting videos once a week so I could focus on quality. I also wanted to have time to share the video after it was posted. When I was posting videos twice a week, I would post the video and then be done, but I was missing huge opportunities. Now after I post my video, I brain-storm on how I can use that video to get more views, rather than spreading myself thin between two videos and trying to keep up with my posting schedule.

Ultimately you want to stay consistent. Once you pick a posting schedule, try to stay committed to it. This means posting on the same days at the same time.

Sharing Your Video

After your video is published, make sure you share it on any social media platforms that you're present on. You can share the video by just sharing the link, sharing the thumbnail, or creating a 15 second version of the video to post on social media, directing people that if they'd like to see more, then they can watch the full video on your YouTube channel.

Another great thing I like to do is join Facebook groups for authors. In those Facebook groups, you'll often find people asking questions, and if one of your videos happens to answer that question, paste it in the comments. Anyone who looks at the comment thread will see your video, which is more potential viewers and subscribers.

There's so many little things you can do to help share your YouTube videos when it comes to social media, but we're going to cover social media in a later book in this series, so be sure to stay tuned!

Getting Discovered - Interacting with the Community

Besides the search engine, another way to be discovered is by integrating yourself in the community. This is more than just responding to people when they comment on your videos. You need to go out and find other AuthorTubers and leave meaningful comment on their videos. Show them that you watched their video and that you think they made great content. Commenting on someone else's videos also opens the door for a possible future collaboration.

Collaborating With Other AuthorTubers

Collaborating with another AuthorTuber is a great way for both of you to connect with a new audience and ultimately you should both benefit from the collab. But it is always best to start connecting with someone before you ask to do a collab.

Even more important than connecting with someone before reaching out to collab, make sure you've spent some time learning how to create videos on your own first.

It's easiest to work with someone else on a YouTube video when you first learn how to make your videos on your own.

There is a bit of a learning curve when you first start your YouTube channel, so make a handful of videos before reaching out to anyone to collaborate. When you do eventually reach out to someone to collaborate, be professional and email them directly. Here are a few things to include in your email:

- Give them a list of a few video topics ideas you have that are similar to topics they've covered on their channel, but they haven't *already* covered.

- Offer a variety of dates for the collab video to go live.

- Mention a method of creating the collab. Will it be planned over email? Will you do a video chat to plan things? Will the videos be filmed separately or will you do a Google Hangout or Skype call to film the videos together? There are many different ways to film a collab video, so make sure you're both clear on the process.

Most of all, please remember collabs are great for building your following, but that's not what it should be about. As I write, I have almost 8,000 subscribers. If I get an email from someone who I've never heard of, who doesn't comment on my videos and who only has 100 subsribers themselves, I'm probably not going to collab with them because...

1. They haven't put in any effort to get to know me or comment on my videos

2. It's hard for me not to assume that they may just be using my following to build their own following.

Make your connections, whether those connections are big or small. But please don't use people just for the sake of building your following. Keep in touch with them, build real friendships, and you'll always be able to reach out to them if you need support.

SEO on YouTube

YouTube is a search engine just like Google. In order for your videos to be noticed, people either need to be subscribed to you already, find the video through search the search engine, or you need to create your videos in a way that the algorithm will pick up the video and suggest it to people to watch.

YouTube is owned by Google, meaning that, just like a blog post needs to be set up in an SEO friendly way, YouTube videos need to do the same. When you upload a video, you need to keep your keywords in mind. This means you should include keywords in your title, description and tags.

Clickable Thumbnails

How do you get someone to click on your video and start watching? Your thumbnail and your title are what attracts people to your video, so make your thumbnail bold and eye-catching. It's best to have yourself featured in that thumbnail. It feels more personal when you see a face on a thumbnail and people are more likely to click.

Canva is a great tool to create graphics, and they even have YouTube thumbnail size templates that you can use to design high-quality thumbnails. Add text and your thumbnails will be looking professional in no time! Of course, like any other tool there is also a paid version of Canva, but the free version should cover everything you'll need!

Expand Your Knowledge

There is so much to know to upload your YouTube videos properly so it gets picked up by the search engine. I could probably write a whole book on how to upload your YouTube video with SEO in mind, but if you'd like to learn more in the subject, join my free AuthorTube Academy Facebook group. In the Facebook group, I post weekly mini-lessons on how to use YouTube. I also like to throw in book marketing advice as well! Join the Facebook group here: http://bit.ly/2JhamHY

In-Depth YouTube SEO

If you enjoy the AuthorTube Academy Facebook group I highly recommend moving on to the full online course, AuthorTube Academy. While the Facebook group has mini-tutorials, AuthorTube Academy is a course I created to help authors learn how to create YouTube videos that will connect with their readers and grow their audience. In the videos, I walk you through exactly how I create and share my videos, step-by-step, as well as cover any other subjects that my students request. Since YouTube is always changing, I add a new video to the course every month. Here's what I've covered in the course so far!

- Creating your YouTube channel

- Designing channel art

- Creating thumbnails with Photoshop & Canva

- Finding topics for your YouTube videos

- Writing your video scripts

- Filming high-quality Youtube videos

- Editing your videos

- Optimizing your videos for SEO

- Writing tags for your video to show up in search

- Getting your video to be a suggested video on YouTube

- Engaging with your audience

- Sharing your video using social media

- Collaborating with other AuthorTubers to grow your channel

- A master list of resources mentioned in the course

- A YouTube checklist that takes you from video to idea to sharing the video online so you don't miss a step

And of course, these are just the tutorials I have so far. The course is always changing and evolving, so be sure to check the website for updates:

AuthorTube Academy:

http://bit.ly/AuthorTube

I would not be where I am today without my YouTube channel. It's brought me many opportunities, from having the courage to publish my first novel, to having the funds to publish every book that's come out since. If you have any curiosity, I encourage you to explore the community and see what you think!

I'll also refere you to a great YouTube channel by Sunny Lenarduzzi, who is a YouTuber that specializes in teaching others the in's and out's of YouTube, social media, and owning a business. Her channel will be linked in the resource section of this book!

TIPS FROM BETHANY:

Just like with blogs, creating a YouTube (AKA AuthorTube) channel is a huge time commitment and one that I wouldn't take lightly.

Ask yourself:

1) would I enjoy this?

2) what is my ultimate purpose for creating video content?

3) can I see myself doing this long term?

In my situation, I hesitated to start an AuthorTube channel because I worried I wouldn't enjoy it. And during the learning curve, when videos took hours upon hours to make, I often didn't. I nearly quit.

But my ultimate purpose for creating content was to reach readers that wouldn't hear of my books otherwise. I knew it was a wonderful place to share my hard work. I also had a secondary reason, which is that I love helping others.

Since I received writing questions on a daily basis (and still do), I felt like this was the best place for me to truly teach and share what I'd learned. Because of those two purposes, I pushed through the learning curve and now really enjoy making videos.

And finally, I'm in it for the long term. This question is important to answer honestly, because you won't see results right away. Just like with writing a book, a YouTube channel takes a lot of time, energy, and patience before you start to see the results of your labor, so definitely ask yourself those questions and take an honest look at if you should pursue AuthorTube or not.

And if you decide to go for it, I definitely recommend checking out Mandi's course, AuthorTube Academy!

CHAPTER 8:
PINTEREST

"Create something people want to share."
—John Jantsch

DID YOU KNOW Pinterest is one of the best ways
to grow your blog? It's an easy way to increase the
traffic on your website with little to minimal effort.
Why does it work? Because Pinterest is a search
engine, just like Google and YouTube. People on
Pinterest are looking for things, so you just need to
make sure your content and your books get in front

of them. And the best way to do this is by creating great pins and engaging content.

Why is it a search engine and not a social network?

You can argue whether Pinterest is a social network or not, but at the end of the day, people go to Pinterest to pin things they like. Most users pin things created by other users, rather than posting their own content. And most importantly, it's not about status updates. It's about the content.

People search for content, which is why it's a search engine rather than a social network. It's not about connecting with one another, it's about finding things.

Pinterest: It's Not Just for DIY Projects

I'm sure when you think of Pinterest, you think of DIY projects, fashion, recipes, and fitness. While these are some of the top categories on Pinterest, they're not the only ones. If you delve into the world of Pinterest as a writer and a reader, you'll discover a whole new world.

Writers pin aesthetics for their works in progress, tips on writing and publishing, and more, such as my personal favorite: what my dream library will look like. If you have a blog, Pinterest should be a priority because you'll easily find a whole new audience there.

Creating Your Account

If you don't already have an account dedicated to writing, then I encourage you to create one now. Make it a business account and link your author website as well as your social media accounts. By verifying your website and social media accounts, any time someone pins something from your website or social accounts, Pinterest will add your logo to the pin. You'll also be able to view analytics to help you see what performs best on Pinterest.

Here's the type of data you'll find with your Pinterest analytics:

- Monthly views of all your profile and pins

- Monthly number of people engaged
- Daily views of your profile and pins
- What people are pinning from your website
- And so much more!

If you make your Pinterest account a business account, you'll have access to some basic analytics. You'll be able to see how your traffic has increased over time, as well as what your top performing pins are. It's important to keep in mind your top performing pins because you want to make note of what performs best on Pinterest. Once you get a few viral pins, you'll notice a pattern, and you'll want to try your best to create more content similar to your top-performing content to help extend your reach even further.

Don't forget to create a short bio for your profile that tells people you're an author and what your blog/website is all about.

Create Your Boards

Once you have your account set up, it's time to start creating your boards. Separate them into writing-related and author-related categories. Make sure you put keywords in the name of your board, as well as the description. Most people miss the fact that your board can have a description, but when you create one, you increase your odds of it showing up in search. Once you have a few pins added to your board, edit the cover of your board to show off your favorite pin or the pin that best exemplifies what the board has for content.

If you want to use your Pinterest account for your own personal pinning as well (because let's face it, we all like to collect our favorite recipes on Pinterest), you could make as many private boards as you'd like! I recommend keeping them private so that people who are following you for your writing-related content don't see your home improvement projects and food recipes. If they see random content in their feed, they may unfollow you.

However, that doesn't mean everything that isn't directly writing has to be kept private. For example, you can pin things related to your writing office, your reading list, inspirational images and quotes, and things of the like!

Let's Get to Pinning!

When it comes to pinning your own content from your blog, you want to make sure a Pinterest-friendly image is embedded within your blog post/webpage, so when someone visits your website, they can easily pin your post on their board.

A great tool to create your images is... you guessed it! Canva! If you read the chapter on YouTube, you already knew this, but let's talk about using Canva specifically for Pinterest!

An ideal Pinterest graphic is 735x1102 pixels and eye-appealing.

Pinterest images should be long rectangles, rather than squares, because that way they get more real estate on Pinterest, thus you're more likely to be seen. If you're struggling for inspiration when it comes to images, just go on Pinterest and see what people with similar content are making.

When you pin your content, make sure you write a description of what the pin/blog post contains for search engine optimization. Throw keywords into your description as well as a few hashtags to make your pins show up better.

Pinning YouTube Videos

Earlier in this book, I mentioned that you can use Pinterest to pin your YouTube videos. YouTube videos pinned on Pinterest don't perform as well as Pinterest images, but there's certainly no harm in pinning the video anyways.

When I upload my YouTube videos, I pin it twice. I pin the video from YouTube, but then I also pin the video embedded on my website as a blog post. At the end of the blog post, I have an image that's different from the imagery I use for my YouTube thumbnail. It's an image customized for each video designed with Pinterest in mind.

Since I don't have a traditional blog, the feed on my blog is actually a feed of all my latest

YouTube videos with a description of what the video is about (which you already know if you read the chapter on blog posts).

After the video description, I embed a Pinterest-friendly image, which allows both myself and my followers to pin the post/YouTube video using that image. This is a great way to take advantage of all the ways you can share your YouTube videos without having to put too much extra effort into it.

While I pin both the video and the image on Pinterest, every time without fail, the image performs better, gets more traffic, and many more re-pins.

Pin, Pin, and Just Keep Pinning!

An important aspect of Pinterest is also pinning other people's content. When you're new to Pinterest, it will be hard to get traction on your own, so make it a personal goal to pin multiple pins a day created by other users. Your goal is to create a great feed of content for your followers. In the beginning, a re-pin on someone else's content is just as good as a re-pin on your own content. At the end of the day, you want to be an account full of quality content, regardless of if it's your content or not.

If you're looking to grow your following and reach on Pinterest, try to make it a goal to re-pin about 10 pins by other users a day to some of your various boards. This will help you attract new followers who will then see the content you create when you throw that in as well.

A well-balanced Pinterest feed is 90% content created by others, while only 10% is content you've created.

It's one of the few platforms where you don't have to worry about having all your content be original. Pinterest accounts thrive on re-pinning content.

When your account gets larger and people start to recognize your brand, you can start pinning more and more of your own content, but as a rule of thumb, it's always best for the majority of what you pin to be what others create.

What Should a Writer's Pinterest Look Like?

Your Pinterest account can be whatever you want it to be. Just like anything else in marketing, I can give you suggestions, but what makes content perform well is what is authentic to you. Pin whatever you want! If you're really stuck, just start following other writers and see what they pin.

Here's some fun board ideas to get you started:

- Novel mood boards & aesthetics:
  - o What images make you think of your novel?
- Writing tips:
  - o You can break it down by advice category to get more bang for your buck!
- Descriptive words:
  - o This sounds weird, but my favorite board I have is called "Getting Wordy" and it's basically my personal thesaurus

when I need help describing something. You could also pin names you like for future characters!

- Libraries:
  - o Book nerds love looking at libraries, and Pinterest is full of them!
- Dream office:
  - o If you could design your office in any way, what would it look like? Pinterest will give you so much office inspiration!
- Books you want to read:
  - o Everyone is always curious what's on your TBR (to be read) list.
- Book marketing tips:
  - o Not only is this great for you to save and reference later, but it is also great for your followers who are writers.
- Publishing tips:
  - o Whether the tips are about self-publishing or traditional publishing, anything that will help another author (and you!) is great to pin.
- Bullet journal spreads:

- o Book lovers and writers tend to be artsy and/or organized. The combination of that is a bullet journal, which is the ultimate form of a planner because the design is all left to you. And where do you go for design ideas? Pinterest.

- Quotes:
  - o Does the quote inspire your novel? Does it inspire you? If it sticks out for any reason, you can pin it!

This is just the start of a very long list of what you can do with Pinterest boards. Do only a few of these things or do all of them! Pinterest should be fun, so don't think too much about it and just start playing around!

Join Group Boards

Group boards on Pinterest are a great way to grow your following. Group boards are an option for a group of Pinterest users to work together to manage one board together. You can either start a group board yourself with friends, or you can request to join a group board that's already been formed. The real thrill of it is that if you're part of a board where the board has more followers than you, than you have direct exposure to those followers when you pin your content.

Keep in mind that it's hard to get on large boards, so start off small. But also know you should vet group boards before you join them. Whatever is pinned to the board, whether you pin it or someone else in the group pins it, it shows up in your feed. A bad group board can do more damage than good. If other members in the group pin inappropriate content it shows up in *your* followers' feeds, even though you weren't the one that made the pin. There are more bad group boards out there than good. Most people abuse them, and as a result, they end up containing a lot of spam and self-advertisement. Your followers will see this, eventually get annoyed by it, and may unfollow you as a result.

On the other hand, a good group board means great pins are being added to the board, thus showing up in your follower's feeds, and as a result, your followers see you as a good resource, even though you didn't have to do the work of finding the pins.

To find group boards, do some searching on http://www.pingroupie.com/ and find boards that are specific to the type of content that you create.

If you struggle to join groups or find quality groups, create your own!

If you know of other authors on Pinterest, contact them and see if they'd be interested in working together on a group board. This way it's with people you trust, and you know the content on the board will be good quality.

I'm part of a group board created by fellow author, Brittany Wang, who added me to her Author Platform and Marketing Tips board. Her rule is that once you post something of your content to the board, that you repost at least two other pins of someone else who's contributed to the board. Most group boards have rules like this, so make sure you read the description of the board before you join.

Tailwind

Pinterest analytics are great, but they're pretty limited. If you want to get more information on the performance of your pins and account, you can to turn to Tailwind, which is made specifically for Pinterest and Instagram, to get full analytics and to schedule posts.

Tailwind's main focus is to schedule pins and Instagram posts. It's an amazing tool for those who are looking to make Pinterest their main marketing focus. Here's a quick view of what Tailwind can help you do on Pinterest:

- Schedule pins
- Know the best time to pin
- Schedule multiple pins at once
- Display Tailwind analytics
- Find your best performing pins of all time

If you're serious about using Pinterest to boost your author platform, I strongly suggest you check out this tool because it can help streamline your time on Pinterest and make growing your presence on Pinterest feel like a walk in the park, if you use it correctly.

If you don't want to use Tailwind, Pinterest recently made an update which allows you to schedule your posts. This means, if you so choose, you can spend one day a week scheduling pins you've created. Pinterest doesn't let you schedule re-pins at this time. Tailwind, on the other hand, does allow you to schedule re-pins.

Personally, I've never used Tailwind for a few reasons. For one, I don't see the need to look further into my analytics. The basic analytics of a Pinterest Business account gives me all the information I need to see which pins perform well and which don't do as well. Would it be cool to look more in-depth into the analytics? Of course! But Tailwind isn't free, so while I'd love to look more into the analytics, I need to budget accordingly, and while analytics is "nice to have" it's not a "must have."

I also don't use Tailwind because I don't have a need to schedule pins. I don't even schedule pins using Pinterest itself. I pin when I want to pin. Pinterest isn't my focus as an author. When I have content that I've already created, why not repurpose it for Pinterest, but it is not where I want to focus my energy.

TIPS FROM BETHANY:

Coming from someone who only used Pinterest for personal pinning for a very long time, it didn't even occur to me that I could add this to the list of awesome ways to sell books!

If, like Mandi said, you see a lot of benefit for reaching readers on Pinterest, then I agree that it'd be wise to make it a priority (especially if you have a blog)!

However, if you're like me and you can see that your audience isn't very present on Pinterest, you still can utilize the platform in small ways to have a presence and reach those outliers who may not find you elsewhere.

For example, I have so many boards unrelated to writing, but I made sure that my board where I'd been saving writing advice was public and slowly began to add my own advice to it, such as YouTube videos I created.

I also took the opportunity to link my Instagram account, where I'm already cultivating pretty photos, to my Pinterest account using an app called IFTTT, so that photos with certain hashtags will post to Pinterest automatically as well.

Finally, once I've published a novel, I make my board full of aesthetics and ideas public so that readers can see and enjoy the photos that inspired that book.

All in all, I put very little time into it, but still have a presence there for anyone who enjoys Pinterest, which makes it a win!

CHAPTER 9:
WHAT'S THE POINT?

"Failure is an option."
—*Matthew Schwartz*

THERE IS NO magic formula to creating the perfect author platform. In fact, I might even go as far as saying your author platform will never be perfect, nor should it be. Just like anything else, you will always strive to do more, to perform better, and to reach more people. That's the goal, right? When you write a book, you don't say you only want 20 people to read it, right? No. You start off with a small goal and then when you reach that goal, you make a new goal, a higher goal.

You'll always reach for more.

You want your book to go as far as it can and if you're willing to put the work into it, you can get there.

I can't give you a step-by-step formula of what will get hundreds of people to sign up to your newsletter, or to get thousands of followers, but I can tell you what I've done. I can tell you what I've learned through working as a content marketer in my full-time job.

But everyone is different, so the process of marketing a book should be different.

When I first started my YouTube channel, I didn't know any of this. I didn't purposely put keywords in my title and description. I didn't share my videos on social media. Heck, I didn't even have social media profiles as an author until my first book was published, despite the fact I started my YouTube channel long before than. I made YouTube videos because I was having fun. I wanted to document my journey. I wanted to make videos about the self-publishing process because at the time, there weren't any videos out there like that. The community we now call AuthorTube didn't exist. My videos caught on by chance, and sometimes that's how things happen. Occasionally, someone creates content and it catches on for no other reason than luck.

But even though sometimes things are left up to chance, knowing how search engines work and how you can encourage people to follow you helps immensely.

Here's what I mean...

I started my YouTube channel in high school. The videos got thousands of views without trying. That was a combination of luck and being one of the first people to cover those types of topics on YouTube.

In college, my YouTube channel was still getting views on my old videos, but my new videos had almost no attention. I still didn't know what I was doing, but now there were other people on YouTube creating similar content to me. I had competition that knew what they were doing and how to show up in search.

It wasn't until I graduated college that I started to figure out how YouTube worked and what I needed to do to catch up and get my YouTube channel back to where it had been.

I made higher-quality videos. My topics were more focused. I was more confident.

I learned how to properly upload the video for search engine optimization. And I started to share the videos on social media as well. It took me a long time to learn how to do everything properly, but when I did learn, something clicked. My YouTube channel, which had turned dormant, was catching on again, and this time it wasn't luck. This time, it was because I knew how the search engine worked.

And did my growing YouTube channel result in growing sales? Yes. It's all about making the world aware that you exist first, and that you have a book second.

So go out and make yourself heard.

Being an author comes with ups and downs, and marketing your book will feel like you're swimming against the current. Trends come and go. You might feel like you're always playing a game of catch-up, but you don't achieve anything unless you try.

Try hard, fail gracefully, and keep moving forward.

That's how you find success.

If this book has helped you in any way, we'd love to hear about it through reviews and tagging us on social media.

Sincerely,

Mandi and Bethany

THANKS FOR READING!
Please leave a short review on Amazon to let us
know what you thought!

http://bit.ly/GrowYourAuthorPlatform

PREORDER THE NEXT BOOK IN
THE SERIES!

Releasing on July 30, 2019!

MARKETING FOR AUTHORS

BOOK
SALES
THAT
MULTIPLY

**Targeting Your Ideal Reader With
eBook Promotions, Paid Ads & More!**

MANDI LYNN
WITH BETHANY ATAZADEH

BE NOTIFIED WHEN THE
PRE-ORDER IS AVAILABLE:

http://bit.ly/marketingforauthors

RESOURCES:

Here are some links from each of the chapters that we think you might find valuable!

Bethany's "Book Marketing for Authors" YouTube Playlist:

http://bit.ly/bookmarketingforauthors

Mandi's "Marketing for Authors" YouTube Playlist:

http://bit.ly/2w3t3aV

Chapter 2 (Your Author Website)

-Brittany Wang's Website Services (Wix): https://www.authorbrittanywang.com/authorwebsitecreator

-Evie Driver's Website Services (Wordpress): https://www.eviedriver.com/

Chapter 3 (Your Email List)

-Mandi's Newsletter:

http://bit.ly/MandisNews

-Bethany's newsletter:

https://www.bethanyatazadeh.com/contact

-MailChimp:

https://mailchimp.com/

-Constant Contact:

https://www.constantcontact.com/

-Hubspot:

https://www.hubspot.com/

-Convert Kit:

https://convertkit.com/

Chapter 5 (Search Engine Optimization)

-Keyword tool, Keywords are Everywhere: https://keywordseverywhere.com/

Chapter 6 (YouTube)

-AuthorTube Academy Free Facebook Group:

http://bit.ly/2JhamHY

-AuthorTube Academy Course:

http://bit.ly/AuthorTube

-Thumbnail creator:

https://www.canva.com/

-Filming Light Mandi Uses: Neewer Dimmable Bi-Color 480 LED Video Light:

https://amzn.to/2D5EDHP

-Travel-Size Filming Light Mandi Uses: LimoStudio 160 LED Video Light:

https://amzn.to/2D55bZU

-Filming Light Bethany Uses: LimoStudio 700W Softbox Lighting Kit:

https://amzn.to/2Ipcejp

-Sunny Lenarduzzi's YouTube Channel:

https://www.youtube.com/sunnylenarduzzi

Chapter 7 (Pinterest)

-Design Pins:

https://www.canva.com/

-Find Pinning Groups:

www.pingroupie.com

-Tailwind (advanced analytics and content scheduling): https://www.tailwindapp.com/

-IFTTT (link different social media accounts for automatic re-posting): https://ifttt.com/

ABOUT THE AUTHORS

ABOUT: MANDI

 *Mandi Lynn* published her first novel when she was seventeen. The author of *Essence*, *I am Mercy*, *She's Not Here*, and the *Marketing For Authors Series*, Mandi spends her days continuing to write and creating YouTube videos to help other writers achieve their dreams of seeing their books published. Mandi is the owner of Stone Ridge Books, a company that works to help authors bring their books to life through cover design and digital book marketing. She is also the creator of AuthorTube Academy, a

course that teaches authors how to grow their presence on YouTube and find loyal readers. When she's not creating, you can find Mandi exploring her backyard or getting lost in the woods.

BOOKS BY MANDI:

 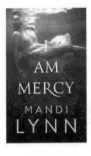 

CONNECT WITH MANDI ON:

Website: https://mandilynn.com

Instagram: @mandilynnwrites

Facebook: @mandilynnwrites

Twitter: @mandilynnwrites

YouTube: www.youtube.com/mandilynnVLOGS

Goodreads: Mandi Lynn

AuthorTube Academy: bit.ly/AuthorTube

AuthorTube Academy Facebook Group:

http://bit.ly/2JhamHY

Mandi's Patreon:

www.patreon.com/mandilynnwrites

ABOUT: BETHANY

Bethany Atazadeh is a Minnesota-based author of *Evalene's Number, Pearl's Number, The Confident Corgi, Penny's Puppy Pack for Writers*, and *How Your Book Sells Itself.* She graduated from Northwestern College in 2008 with a Bachelor of Arts degree in English with a writing emphasis. After graduation, she pursued songwriting, recording, and performing with her band, and writing was no longer a priority. But in 2016, she was inspired by the NaNoWriMo challenge to write a novel in 30 days, and since then she hasn't stopped. She is passionate about God, her husband, writing, music, and dogs, specifically her Corgi puppy, Penny.

BOOKS BY BETHANY:

 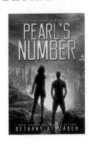 

CONNECT WITH BETHANY ON:

Website: www.bethanyatazadeh.com

Instagram: @authorbethanyatazadeh

Facebook: @authorbethanyatazadeh

Twitter: @bethanyatazadeh

YouTube: www.youtube.com/bethanyatazadeh

Goodreads: Bethany Atazadeh

Patreon: www.patreon.com/bethanyatazadeh

Printed in Great Britain
by Amazon